AMERICAN

SERIES EDITOR, EDWARD FOLEY

LITURGICAL LANGUAGE

Keeping It Metaphoric, Making It Inclusive

GAIL RAMSHAW

A Liturgical Press Book

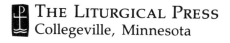

THE LITURGICAL PRESS
Collegeville, Minnesota

Cover design by Ann Blattner

1   2   3   4   5   6   7   8

Library of Congress Cataloging-in-Publication Data

Ramshaw, Gail, 1947–
    Liturgical language : keeping it metaphoric, making it inclusive /
Gail Ramshaw.
      p.   cm. — (American essays in liturgy)
    ISBN 0-8146-2408-1
    1. Catholic Church—Liturgy. 2. Catholic Church—United States—
Liturgy. 3. Liturgical language—English. 4. Metaphor—Religious
aspects—Catholic Church. 5. Nonsexist language—Religious
aspects—Catholic Church. 6. Sexism in liturgical language. I. Title.
II. Series: American essays in liturgy (Collegeville, Minn.)
BX1970.R34 1996
264'.02—dc20   95-33193
                                                 CIP

Contents

1 The Challenge for Liturgical Language

What is meant by "liturgical language"?

This essay uses the term "liturgical language" to refer to the words used by assemblies of Christians in their corporate praise and prayer. Liturgical language is not the whole of the vocabulary of the Christian faith. Mystics speak and write in words and syntax less tamed, more idiosyncratic, more fragmented, than can be the speech of public worship. Systematic theologians write language more philosophical, speculative or argumentative than a typical assembly could tolerate. While liturgical language is only one of several types of Christian speech, it can be argued that it is the essential and primary speech, the basic language from which all other speech flows in exposition and reflection and to which, when Sunday comes around again, all Christian talk returns.[1]

The precise list of words, phrases, and forms in the language of liturgy varies from one denomination to another. In some Christian communities, the words admitted to Sunday worship are prescribed by past tradition or by contemporary authorities. All the appropriate words are written down, and all the participants, including all leaders of worship, read or recite their parts with no variation. In other communities, the particular congregation or perhaps the ordained minister has the continual task of reviewing and selecting texts for public worship. But even where improvised prayer is expected, rather than forbidden, it will not be long before a particular denomination or assembly regularizes a pattern for preferred improvisation. One way or another, a canon of words will be approved for corporate worship and will constitute the liturgical language of that community.

Within that canon of words and phrases will be a hierarchy of significance. Some words will be absolutely essential to the community's self-definition. The phrase "The body of Christ," said at the Communion, exemplifies those words without which the assembly could not rehearse its origin, its meaning, and its goal. Some words, like the biblical echoes in hymns and chants—one thinks of "Lamb of God, you take away the sin of world"—are so sanctified by tradition and so multivalent in meaning that their place in liturgical language is secured. Some words and images are optional: a community may include or exclude from its worship hymns with battle imagery that construes life as a war against evil and Christ as the commander of the troops. Most Christians craft the intercessions newly each week, with more or less direction to the writer as to the content or the style. At the bottom of the hierarchy in sacred speech, so far down that some people omit them from the scale altogether, are the announcements. Yet for better or for worse they play an important role in many assemblies and ought not be to ignored: what is ignored is not analyzed, understood, and improved.

Not only does each Sunday morning contain a hierarchical range of liturgical words; the seasons of the liturgical year present another range of holy texts. Some ritual phrases are like the solstice, necessarily coming around every year. Examples are the text of baptism or the responses at the Easter Vigil. Others are occasional and optional, such as a particular hymn or the prayers at private confession and absolution. Thus the whole body of liturgical language is less like an index, a list of words in alphabetical order, and more like a tree, with some words as essential as the trunk, and others as seasonal as autumn colors or as short-lived as that one single leaf.

Like a tree, liturgical language grows. In those communities in which change is slow—the redwoods among us—there has been translation from parent languages. This most mammoth change has occurred at least once even for linguistically conservative Christians, for example the Ethiopic Churches who pray in Ge'ez and the Slavic assemblies who use Church Slavonic. Many mainline Christian Churches in the United States are more like dogwoods, changing colors each season and growing noticeably each year, hoping to avoid the blight which is always ready to attack. In small or in substantial ways, each Christian community must decide how its liturgical language is to grow. How must the language change in order for the meaning to be authentically conveyed? Which words must stay the same for identity to be preserved? At which ecclesiastical level are these decisions best made? What if we judge that the decisions made for us are wrong? The direction, the pace, and the process of change and growth are all debatable issues.

The nature of the changes may differ from one decade to another. In the middle of this century, many Christian Churches were engaged in a monumental translation project. Roman Catholics and some Orthodox Churches went from Latin and other medieval languages to the vernacular, while Protestant Churches replaced sixteenth-century English with twentieth. Many people believed that the language of the marketplace was unable to carry the sacred resonance of the uniquely holy speech of public worship. The task for those decades was to find the balance between the otherness of speech necessary for speaking about God and the ordinariness of language necessary for describing the incarnation. God, for whom extraordinary speech is appropriate, is born in a stable and in all baptized persons, about whom quite ordinary words are required. Christianity, unlike for example Orthodox Judaism or Hinduism, avoids a wholly other sacral speech, a language reserved solely for holy things. Rather, since before the writing of the New Testament, the Church translated and translated again, in order to bring the holy into the ordinary so that the ordinary could be seen as holy. No one ever claimed that this is an easy linguistic task.

The Churches' task at the close of the twentieth century is a different one, although it is similarly a balancing act between two opposite goods. Liturgical language must be crafted so as to be both metaphoric and inclusive, and it is this complex and controverted issue that this essay addresses.

Metaphor the method

In order for human language to talk about God, it requires metaphor. The American poet Wallace Stevens described metaphor as the tension produced by talking about two different things at the same time.[2] Metaphor is that use of speech in which the context demonstrates that a factually or logically inaccurate word is on the deepest level true. The wrong word is seen to be the right word; to talk about X, we use the image of Y. In a poem of resignation, Emily Dickinson wrote, "Life is over there—Behind the Shelf."[3] Literally it is not, metaphorically it is. Living metaphor always surprises, for in the moment of tension the human imagination discovers that the odd word is more profoundly true than factual description. About his novels William Faulkner quipped, "I tell the truth. When I need a fact, I make it up."[4] Readers find in the metaphors that Faulkner invented deeper truths about the American experience than can be conveyed through a newspaper report or videotape.

Metaphor bends reality into odd twists and turns. Metaphor is not only a new look at reality, a slight of the mind: it is also multivalent. One reason metaphor can be more true than fact is that it contains many layers of meaning simultaneously. God is "in heaven," says Christian metaphor, and to explicate this factually deceptive if not false statement, we would need layers and layers of truth, some available to the toddler, some open to catechumens, some reached only after decades of sorrow and joy in the Christian community. A multivalent metaphor opens up an archeological dig, available for exploration at whichever level each believer can undertake.

Christian linguistic philosophers have long struggled with the untruth of metaphor. How is it possible that the Church asserts that it believes something demonstrably untrue? In dealing with this paradox, Thomas Aquinas taught a distinction between metaphor and analogy.[5] Metaphor, he judged, is common in Christian speech but ultimately dispensable. "God is a rock" is an example of such speech; although it can lead to truth, it is inaccurate and finally unnecessary. Better, Aquinas said, is analogy, words like "God is good," in which the very definition of "good" proceeds not from human imagination and earthly parallel, but from scriptural revelation. Thus Aquinas and contemporary Thomists explore metaphor, but, wary of its inaccuracy, relegate it to secondary status.[6]

A similar delineation, separating more accurate language from less, is found in the argument of Roland Frye and other conservative Protestant scholars who warn against recent or contemplated changes in liturgical language.[7] Not comfortable with the category of analogy, these writers contrast what they call metaphor, such as "God is father," with what they call simile, such as "God as mother." According to this distinction, metaphor is a figure of speech more fully true, a simile one only partially appropriate. The literary labels have shifted since Aquinas, but the Christian quest remains the same: to understand how Christian speech uses inaccurate speech in proclaiming truth and to rationalize the inclusion of metaphor in creed.

One way to appreciate the quarrels of the sixteenth-century

Church is to realize that linguistic analysis was changing.[8] How did the words of the faith have their meaning? Martin Luther would not have agreed with Thomas Aquinas about how language functioned. Was medieval philosophy correct in postulating an ontological truth in naming, or was a developing modernism more accurate in seeing words as arbitrary labels? What kind of speech is the phrase "The body of Christ for you"? The modern world, less able than earlier Christian centuries to accept a connection between the divine and the human, could not rely on the truth of any of its words.

Scientific verification and its consequent development, fundamentalism, have introduced into the discussion further complications.[9] The fathers and mothers of the Church assumed and taught that the deepest truth of a biblical passage was other and deeper than its literal meaning. One example of this Christian bias toward metaphor is seen in Augustine's *Confessions*: Augustine began to pay serious attention to the gospel only when he encountered Ambrose's preaching, in which the literal interpretation of scriptural passages, which Augustine judged to be naive and ignorant, was replaced by the symbolic.[10] Yet many Christians, influenced by scientific procedures, are reversing this tradition by searching for literal descriptions of God's truth for them.

The premier scholar of metaphor in our time, Paul Ricoeur, has helped liturgists see why liturgical language is and must be metaphoric.[11] With all due respect to Aquinas, contemporary theorists conclude that metaphor is not dispensable. Rather, it is the distinctive characteristic of the working human mind. To see something newly; to suggest that it is as it is not and in the suggestion to make it so for the community; to expand human imagination by the layering of what is with what was not: this is the process of human thought and the vehicle of human communication. Although some speech is more obviously metaphoric than other, all extension of thought and all accumulation of imagination are at root metaphoric endeavors. We recognize this use of the mind when the three-year-old after a long bath looks in dismay at her toes and cries out, "I got raisin feet!"; when scientists call something, perhaps a collapsed star, a black hole; and when in the psalmist's laments, the dogs snarl around and the wild bulls lower their horns for attack. For Ricoeur, such creativity of the mind shaping and nurturing communal meaning is what Genesis means by "the image of God."[12] The divine has burst out from the natural; meaning has been created.

Ricoeur teaches that words in isolation have no discernible meaning.[13] Words have meaning only within a specific context and within a specific community of discourse. This is extremely significant for crafters of liturgical language. The phrase ''a man born blind'' can refer to a male we know who was born sightless, and the context will go on to comment on his Braille skills. However, ''a man born blind'' can also refer to every human being before baptism, the context being a discussion of the Lenten catechumenate. Neither sentence contains the ''correct'' use of the words. For Ricoeur, this ambivalence is not an unfortunate problem, but the joyous matrix of human communication: meaning, because metaphoric, occurs always and only in context.

Metaphor is the method of liturgical language. To say the unknowable God and to describe mercy, the community relies on metaphor. ''May God's face shine upon you,'' we say. Of course, God has no face. But we give God a face as part of the way we say mercy. May it ''shine'': another metaphor. The Church is continuously cultivating its garden of metaphors. Which ones are coming along just fine, producing healthy fruits and flowers? What needs a little manuring? What is dying on the vine and no longer befits the garden? The hope is that with all the metaphors thriving, meaning will abound for all the faithful. Wallace Stevens' poem ''Thirteen Ways of Looking at a Blackbird'' is supposedly about only blackbirds: yet each successive statement layers up meaning until the reader feels that all of the world has been seen.[14] Like Stevens' blackbird, the ''face'' of God means more than we first thought.

Inclusivity the goal

Here's the wrinkle: liturgy is not poetry. Liturgy includes the communal recitation of the central metaphors of the faith, but liturgy is grounded in the assembly in a way that most poetry is not. The liturgy is the expression of all the people of God, and all those people need to have their voices heard. This goal we call here inclusivity.

The daily prayer of the devout Jewish male gives thanks that he is not a heathen, not a slave, and not a woman. Perhaps this characteristic religious tendency to separate the insiders from the outsiders, the sacred from the profane, was the foil behind Paul's radical manifesto that in Christ there is no difference between Jew and Greek, slave and free, male and female. But although this inclusivity may have been the goal of the primitive Christian community, two thousand years has not yet brought the Church there. The New Testament chronicles the Church's struggles to see Jew and Greek as equal before God. Only in the last few hundred years has a consensus of Christians seen "slave and free" as a distinction inappropriate within the Christian community, and in our time the distinction between male and female is the tumult of the Church. Paul's extraordinary vision would encourage a liturgy enacted without distinction of race and class, unmarked by economic divisions, and free from androcentrism.

Such inclusivity is not only a beacon shining from our past: it is also a major political movement of the age. Am I getting my rights? Has my group been included? The movement has tumbled totalitarian governments; it has been soaked in the blood of neighboring tribes. Both inside and outside democracies, the individual's hopes for a better future have revolutionized vocabulary and called for massive re-education. Native and African Americans wish to speak for themselves, no longer allowing Anglo-Americans to do the talking. The dispossessed cry out their distress, and women refuse to be silent. All of us are speaking for ourselves.

The difference between the classic Christian gift of the voice and the contemporary demand to be heard is that ideally in the Church we gladly yield the floor. All of us try to articulate, not our own need, but the need of others. Such is the goal particularly of the intercessory prayer. The intercessions are not meant to be either a personal or communal wish list or a set of resolutions summarizing the preaching. Rather, in the intercessions the Church gives voice to all the voiceless, praying for all the needy who are not present, and trusting that God's inclusive salvation will come for the whole world.

An oxymoron

Grammarians define an oxymoron as two opposite words juxtaposed, two ideas that only in paradox can sit side by side. "A living death" is an oxymoron, so is "metaphoric inclusivity." A metaphor suggests a huge truth by means of a single mental twist. Inclusive speech calls for a precise listing of the situations of all the people, who are thus able to speak for themselves. "Females and males, infants and middle-aged, disabled and able-bodied, Hindu and New Age pagan, a Baptist youth and an adult convert"—such is a partially inclusive list of those coming to baptism. But metaphorically the gospel says only "a man born blind."

The investigation of this oxymoron is the focus of this essay. How can the liturgical language of our assemblies be both metaphorical and inclusive? How can the language pour down past centuries of Christian imagination and also spring up to articulate contemporary needs? When the goals seem not only paradoxical but downright antithetical, which principle guides which part of the liturgy? When must metaphors be discarded or replaced because current sensibilities hear them as offensively exclusive? When does metaphor offer a deeper inclusivity than any list we could assemble? Some people lean too far toward metaphor, not very concerned that all voices be heard; others lean too far towards inclusivity, unable to program their computers to produce metaphors and accustomed to the flattened babble of E-mail.

Fortunately the sentences we are crafting are long sentences, stretching through the liturgy of Sunday morning, across our devotions, occasional services, and paraliturgical exercises of the week, through the year from one Advent to another, and from one decade of our common life to the next. Each sentence needs the sentences before and after for balance, clarity, and correction; each Sunday needs the next Sunday, a slightly different light cast on the gem of the cross. Perhaps even one denomination, expert in metaphor, needs another, alert to inclusivity, for mutual maturation in the body of Christ.

2 Our Linguistic History

Implications of a translation religion

Christian liturgical language is rooted in prebiblical sacred rhetoric. The Semitic tribes who in later centuries were known as the Jews borrowed from other peoples words for the deity, for good and for evil. It is probably anachronistic to think of the early Israelite tribes as religiously distinctive from the other tribal groups of the ancient Near East. For example, both the divine names El Shaddai and YHWH were in use before we hear of their being revealed to Abraham and Moses.[15] It appears that although the biblical writers came to reject absolutely the deities deemed efficacious by their neighbors, sacred power that was already on the wane was more easily incorporated into the Israelite tradition. Thus El, the Canaanite creator deity resting in retirement, became one of the names of the Hebrew God, while Baal and Asherah, actively worshipped by many Canaanites, were rejected and, according to the ferocious story in 1 Kings, their prophets assassinated.

The name El Shaddai offers a typically complex example of this appropriation of religious vocabulary. Originally naming a deity who was worshipped in the Transjordan, the word Shaddai is a metaphor referring either to the distant mountains on which the god resides or the twin peaks of the goddess's breasts.[16] But when in the Greco-Roman world the Jews translated their Scriptures into Greek, they rendered the name El Shaddai as Pantokrator, "Almighty God," thus replacing the ancient and obscure natural metaphor with contemporaneous philosophical monotheism.

One might use this example to rue the results of translation. Indeed, some religions are so aware of the uniqueness of the original

13

language that formed their tradition that they refuse translation. Orthodox Jews worship in ancient Hebrew; Muslims decry translation of Qur'an. Some Christians have not attended to new liturgical translation for over a millennium: the Ethiopians worship in Ge'ez, the Egyptians pray in Coptic. The religious conservatives among us rightly warn of the losses suffered in any translation.

But despite the possibility of losing metaphor or distorting meaning, Christianity for the most part follows the biblical pattern of continuous translation. Let us consider the example of Wisdom.[17] It is likely that not only the influence of the tribe's old wise women, but also the Egyptian power of justice, Maat, stand behind the Hebrew hypostasis of divine wisdom, Hokmah. Undoubtedly a Canaanite goddess and the Greek goddess of wisdom also influenced the late Jewish poetry in which Hokmah has been transmogrified into the great Sophia in the skies. Paul's encounter with the risen Christ led him to call Christ Sophia, but it is the Johannine community, by transferring the feminine-gendered Sophia into the masculine-gendered Logos, who secured the metaphor of divine wisdom for Christianity. Maat, Isis, Anat, Athena, Sophia, the Logos, all come to the cross through the technique of translation. Centuries later Christians continue the pattern: Should we retrieve a feminine-gendered Sophia? What is gained and what is lost by adding yet another layer?

Each layer of translation, each choice of a new category nearly congruent with the old, loses a bit of the old, perhaps for good, perhaps for ill, and adds to the accumulated meaning something from outside, again perhaps for good, perhaps for ill. In the phrase "the Body of Christ for you," the "you" was always plural. Since English no longer has two forms of "you," one singular and one plural, its plural theological intent is unclear in English liturgical use. Current interest in individuality has brought about the phenomenon that on Sunday morning one hears "For you, Suzie . . . For you, Jim." Is this alteration from plural to singular for good or for ill? Translation, whether from Egyptian into ancient Hebrew, from Hebrew into Greek, or from nineteenth to twenty-first century English, adds a layer. Another floor has been added to the structure, but the congruence is never perfect.

Ideally, metaphor is inclusive. The Christian Logos has embraced the Egyptian idea of justice, the Canaanite goddess, the Hebrew idea of wisdom, the Greek goddess of wisdom, the philosopher's notion of divine emanation, and finally the death of Christ. The cen-

14

tral idea grew to include one culture after another. Unfortunately the layers tend to be squashed by later weight: few contemporary Christians know much about the philosophical category of Logos and so cannot appreciate its rendering of Sophia or its importance in the Trinitarian language of God as Son. The translation task is never over for Christians. The very words we speak change in connotation, even denotation, year by year, and in order to proclaim the incarnation, we must speak the gospel in words that the shepherds in our fields can understand.

Already in the New Testament the early Church discarded the idea that the resurrection is meant for only one ethnic group. Christianity, as a voluntary religious organization, required evangelistic fervor and learned other languages so as to speak the gospel. For whatever reasons, linguistic archaisms came to have little place in Christianity. Paul, when writing in Greek to Greeks, does cite the Aramaic Abba as a word for prayer (Rom 8:15; Gal 4:6). But Abba did not remain a key word in Christian vocabulary. It was translated, although of course not precisely. Maranatha, once significant, also faded. Except for a few words—Amen, Hallelujah—the Church tries to speak the vernacular. One of the several considerable impediments in rendering YHWH as Yahweh in liturgical speech is that reintroducing an archaism moves against the spirit of Christian liturgical language. The dominant Christian idea is that God's grace is proclaimed in every tongue, to be heard by all, not excluding those unacquainted with an esoteric code speech. Translation is the fundamental technique available to liturgical language for its task of inclusivity.

The development of English

The earliest form of what became U.S. English is called either Old English or Anglo-Saxon and existed in several dialects in England from about 700 to 1100. It arose, scholars speculate, from a subdivision of the original proto-Indo-European speech. Like its cousins German, Frisian, Flemish, and Dutch, Anglo-Saxon was a fully inflected language, with changes in pronunciation (e.g., mouse-mice) and form (e.g., to be, am, is, are, was, were, has been, have been) to indicate number, tense, and grammatical usage. Since Anglo-Saxon was so heavily inflected and employed several letters no longer extant in our alphabet, it is no longer comprehensible to the

15

casual reader. *Fæder ure þu þe eart on heofonum, ūrne gedæghwamlican hlāf syle us to dæg* was how the West Anglo-Saxon Christians prayed "Our Father in heaven, give us today our daily bread."[18] Contemporary students find the language closer to modern German or Dutch than to modern English.

After the Norman invasion in 1066, Anglo-Saxon became the language of the uneducated, and by the time it reemerged as Middle English in the thirteenth century, its inflections had been radically simplified. Although one must learn Anglo-Saxon in order to read it, one can muddle through Middle English—the language of Chaucer and of Julian of Norwich[19]—without study. One characteristic evident in the move from Anglo-Saxon to Middle English and from Middle to modern English is the continuing simplification of inflections and endings. In our time, for example, the precise use of the apostrophe in plurals and possessives seems to be eluding many Americans, and the *-ess* feminine ending of words like *poetess* is being abandoned. The latest biblical translations name Miriam a prophet, not any longer a prophetess.

Anglo-Saxon utilized metaphor to create new words. The cross of Christ could be rendered with the word *rod* or with the metaphor *sigebeam*, "victory-tree." The tribal authority was termed *hlāford*, an elision from the metaphor *hlāf*, "loaf of bread," and *weard*, "ward" or "guardian." This metaphoric tendency, so spellbinding for the student of Anglo-Saxon, was much diminished in Middle English. *Hlāford* was further elided into lord, its metaphoric meaning obscured by its connotation of economic dominance and social privilege.

A second characteristic of the development of English has been toward precision. Dictionaries brought standardized spelling, the academy taught approved grammar, and the scientific revolution required accuracy in labeling. Information technology has yet again both simplified existing words ("electronically-sent messages" becomes "E-mail") and exponentially multiplied new categories. Let no one suggest, however, that language has lost the metaphoric method in the naming of new concepts: If you use your mouse to double-click on an icon to open a window, you speak metaphorically. Recent pride in regional speech and a breakdown of taboos have sharply increased the amount of slang, which by definition is emotive and imprecise speech (although slang moves quickly toward either shared clarity or oblivion).

The moves toward simplification and precision are of greatest import for liturgical language. Anglo-Saxon, along with other Germanic languages, operated with grammatical gender, a system of noun and pronoun classification with attendant inflected endings. In Anglo-Saxon, *rod*, "cross," was feminine; *sigebeam*, "victory-tree," was masculine; *wif*,"woman," was neuter. Scholars have identified precisely during which decades this grammatical gender was abandoned.[20] In a chronicle kept by the monks of Peterborough, the entries in 1131 were written in accurate Anglo-Saxon. After a twenty-year gap, when the writing resumed in 1154, grammatical gender, some declensions, and some conjugations had disappeared. Middle English simplified the gender system towards the modern English pattern that gender denotes only natural sex. Thus only when speaking in outmoded archaisms can one in contemporary American English call the Church "she." The implications for liturgical language of English rejecting grammatical gender are substantial.

Let this short history of the English language suffice to ground our discussion of liturgical language in the specifics of our speech. Speakers of different languages will by necessity see different aspects of the current controverted questions. Not surprisingly, a British citizen hears language of royalty and kingship differently than a U.S. citizen does, and a country that still has lords registers the word differently than does our own. Complicating the task for the Church is the desire that Christians around the world be able to speak to one another. It is true that every change required or desired by Christian speakers of contemporary American English may move their proclamation of the faith some small or considerable distance from that heard in another part of the world. Yet the task of application remains before the Church.

Granting that liturgical language is both metaphoric and inclusive and that English is progressively simplifying its grammar and expanding toward precision, we examine three type of issues of liturgical language: so-called generic speech, symbolic imagery, and the conventions the Church has utilized in identifying God. We mean not to offer specific replacements for each controverted word, but rather to suggest the principles by which the next generation of Christians will guide their choices to attain speech that is both metaphoric and inclusive.

3 Generic Speech

Synecdoche, convention, or misogyny?

Students of rhetoric use the classic Greek term synecdoche to refer to a metaphor in which a part stands for the whole. In synecdoche, as in all metaphor, more is implied than what is said. When Israel's salvation is credited to God's "mighty hand and outstretched arm," both personification—describing something as human which is not—and synecdoche have been employed: God's entire power is indicated by only God's hand and arm. A hymn that praises Christ's scepter employs synecdoche, the scepter standing for an entire panoply of royal prerogatives. It has been argued that so-called generic speech is poetic synecdoche. A poem could say "man" when it means all of humankind: the line will scan easier, and the smaller entity stands for and brings with it the greater.

Some people have argued that generic speech is linguistic convention. Native speakers in a language are usually unaware of their conventions, although those learning the language are well aware of short cuts in current usage. By convention, we answer "I don't think so," when what we actually mean is "I think it is not so"; we ought never admit that we "do not think"! Proponents of generic speech as linguistic convention point to the 1850 British Act of Parliament in which "he" was said to stand for "he or she" in all future official proceedings, a decision enacted largely to simplify the minutes, but cited by linguistic conservatives as proof that male speech as inclusive of the female is linguistic convention in English.

This linguistic convention indicates an androcentric worldview that takes males (*andr-* is the Greek root for "male") as central to the system. According to this worldview, the male is the prototypical human, perhaps created first, perhaps rationally superior, perhaps physically more muscular, perhaps legally or economically or morally the free agent. Such androcentrism may be defended as reflecting God's will or as ensuring social stability, or it may be partially or wholly decried. The nineteenth-century Quaker Sarah Grimke demonstrated an early American rejection of androcentrism when she argued from the Genesis 1 story of both male and female being made in the image of God that men were not ontologically, legally, or ethically superior to women.[21] Yet such androcentrism is not easily purged from language.

Many contemporary feminists have gone one step further, seeing in generic speech conscious or unconscious misogyny. They suggest that hatred of women (*gyn-* is the Greek root for "female") was once, has always been, or continues to be the foundation for a speech pattern that dismisses women or subsumes them as silent supporters of a statement made by men. Feminist Christians argue that even if some aspects of the social order and its speech are androcentric, the Christian faith must reject misogyny and work towards equality in language and life.[22]

Androcentric speech in the liturgy

Liturgical language has traditionally been loaded with androcentric speech. Already in the Bible God is the deity of the patriarchs; the names of sons are recorded more often than those of daughters; male disciples are named individually, while female disciples are often grouped together; apostolic letters and sermons assume a male audience; God is routinely likened to a male, only rarely to a female.[23] Feminist biblical scholars have demonstrated that the Hebrew and Greek texts seldom make clear whether or not a corporate noun includes women.[24] Thus whether any group, for example "the crowd" or "the elders," includes women is not apparent. The European languages that are precursors to American English were all androcentric. Thus virtue (*vir* is Latin for "man") is a desirable quality, and hysteria (*hystera* is Greek for "womb") is uncontrolled irrationality.[25] This androcentric bias spread out throughout prayers, preaching, and hymnody. A lively debate has been raging over the past decades as to whether such androcentric speech—"for us *men* and for our salvation," "may *his* face shine upon us"—is synecdoche, convention, or misogyny.

The achievement of optimal status of women and of men in the Church may be a universal Christian ideal, but the languages in which Christians pray for that day are particular. The arbiters of American English—activist lexicographers, textbook editors, the style sheets of major newspapers, high-visibility broadcasters, politicians seeking re-election—have steadily worked to avoid and even expunge not only androcentric speech but also gender stereotypes from our language. The major publishers of elementary school textbooks disallow not only what used to be standard "generic" speech, but also stereotypical gender depictions in the accompanying art.[26] A primary reader already in 1980 depicted "Old Macdonald" as an old woman on her farm. In 1976 the National Council of Teachers of English voted that it is preferable to say "Each of them handed in their papers" rather than the traditionally taught "Each handed in his paper."[27] It may be that other languages are proceeding along different paths, but the future of American English is clear: thoughtful usage will excise historic generic speech.[28]

It is not surprising that generic speech has lost credence. Male terminology included women only when it chose to. Indeed, as Paul Ricoeur reminded us, the word "man" has no unequivocal meaning outside a specific context. Analysis demonstrates that benign statements about men, such as "All men are created equal" or "Christ forgives all men their sins," were inclusive of women. However, statements about rights or privileges were not inclusive: a century ago, statements like "All men can vote" or "Christian men can seek ordination" did not include women. "Men" was not in fact a generic term, but meant males or males and females depending on the context.

In a world in which increasingly the roles and rights of males and females are at issue, generic speech can no longer be employed by those who hope their language will be clear and inoffensive. Careful speakers of American English recast their sentences now, since inattention to these matters creates ambiguity. Far from being inclusive, generic speech was doubly exclusive, both in that it often meant only males and in that only the insiders knew when the word meant what.

Liturgical language includes both translations of texts from the Christian past and newly composed texts. The abandonment of the fiction of generic speech requires two tasks of liturgists: the arduous work of retranslating the Bible, the ordinary of the liturgy, and the massive collection of accompanying texts, such as proper prayers and hymns; and the creative effort to craft intercessions, homilies, new hymns, and all devotional and paraliturgical materials in a newly emerging American English that is both genuinely inclusive and aesthetically graceful.[29] It may be that assemblies will allow some archaic androcentrisms to remain in, for example, hymns composed in an earlier form of English. But such retention will be ethical only if the archaisms are recognized as such and no longer are practiced and defended as acceptable current usage.

Pronouns for God

A controversial instance of such generic speech in the liturgy has been the use of masculine pronouns for God. Despite some rare female imagery for God surfacing now and then in the Bible and through subsequent tradition, until recent decades the Christian God has been called ''he'' exclusively in the liturgy. Under attack, this practice is now being defended with various arguments which require our attention.

First it must be acknowledged that most Christians who called God ''he'' never had to defend this speech because such usage was not analyzed or challenged. In contrasting Christianity with Gnosticism, Gregory of Nazianzus (in a rare moment in the ancient Christian tradition) clarified that his use of ''he'' did not mean to suggest that God is masculine.[30] But most of the tradition adopted the usage unconsciously.

Some have argued that ''he'' is in some way essential to God-language, that it is in some way true, or at least more accurate than any other pronoun. For those Christians who adopt an Aristotelian model of human beings, in which males have more rationality than females, God, as sheer rationality, must be more like human males than human females.[31] The opposite position is now occasionally suggested: that God is in essence more like a female than a male and thus ought to be called ''she.''[32] The problem with either extreme in this essentialist argument is that to maximize differences between men and women,[33] they must be described in terms highly subjective, culturally determined, and scientifically debatable. On the basis of gender descriptions perhaps exaggerated (and in the case of Aristotle's, biologically erroneous), claims are made about God's essence which in turn is supposed to influence human behavior. The circularity of the argument does not commend it.

21

Some have argued that religions in which God is not "he" rely on patterns of thought incompatible with the Christian faith.[34] "He" is thus the polemical preference for some who treasure the uniqueness of the Christian message. Among these are some who argue that rejection of Canaanite goddesses was behind the use of the masculine pronoun for YHWH in the Hebrew Scriptures.[35] Others cite the current revival of the pantheistic wicca and see an evangelistic necessity that the Christian God be "he."[36] It is true that Christian faith must make clear what it is not. Yet theology must also guard that its negative statements do not result in misrepresentations. To teach that God is not a certain "she" does not require an assertion that God is a certain "he."

Some have argued, just as with other androcentric usage, that speaking of God as "he" is linguistic convention. Our religious tradition, and the English language in describing monotheism, has always said "he." Some assert that it is important to maintain traditional speech, others that our language provides no option. These arguments see no essential truth in the masculine pronoun but still defend its status in the tradition. For these people, the tasks of retranslating all inherited texts and reformulating all future speech are so colossal as to be impossible to attempt, even ridiculous to contemplate. Not surprisingly, when there is no will, no way is seen.

Yet another variation is heard in those who argue that while "he" is not essentially true of God, it is metaphorically appropriate. For some it is the only pronoun that is appropriate.[37] Some grant occasional use of "she" or "it," for example for the Spirit, but defend "he" as the most appropriate pronoun.[38] In general, this position derives from the maximizing argument, for it relies on some identifiable, albeit not biological, distinction between males and females, with categories somehow appropriate to God.

As the Church comes to take seriously the inclusivity of its liturgical language, use of "he" for God will increasingly be recognized as problematic, if not indefensible. Until more data than our own cultural stereotypes and prejudices are in, claims about essential predispositions of each gender can be only hesitantly proposed. Cementing any such proposals into God-language is presumptuous and only perpetuates stereotypes that curtail inclusivity. A linguistic system in which males are rulers and females are nannies is no more inclusive than one in which whites are rulers and blacks are nannies. As the androcentric pronoun system comes to be examined as closely as have been our androcentric "generic" nouns, "he" for God will be more and more abandoned and its replacement with one grammatical construction or another will become natural.

We cannot forget, however, that liturgical language relies on metaphor. Since the essence of God is unknowable, all talk of God must tell only what God is like. Any serious consideration of such speech demonstrates that God is also unlike our best attempts at comparison. As the Fourth Lateran Council said it, in all our speech about God, what is unlike is always greater than what is like.[39] Metaphoric speech about God might allow use of both "he" and "she," with an occasional "it." The psalter gives ample examples of praise to a God who is somehow like a warrior, a judge, a lamp. Similarly, God is somehow like a he, a she, an it. The concern for inclusivity would require some balance between the options.

But even the metaphoric meaning of God as "he" or "she" remains a quandary. Given an androcentric tradition and a still sexist society, the metaphors that come automatically to mind—God as king is he, God as mother is she—seem inevitably to construe the male as somehow the superior and dominant gender. One advantage of the revival of the image of God as a female Wisdom is that such a "she" is a figure of might, authority, judgment, beneficence, bearing a regal power seldom assigned feminine gender.

Perhaps the most inclusive, while still metaphoric, use of pronouns for God is to interchange "he" with "she" indiscriminately when the context allows and no confusion results. American Lutherans have kept alive a seventeenth-century hymn entitled "Whatever God ordains is right."[40] The four stanzas each contain six statements about God which stress biblical verbs: God, "in whom alone is gladness," "leads us in the way of light and will never leave us," "heals our souls and gives us sight." Interchanging "she" with "he" in this hymn's twenty-four phrases creates no semantic confusion, since the referent is clear. Yet by allowing the worshippers to imagine queens and kings, aunts and uncles, mothers and fathers, the pronouns enlarge the verbs. In such a case the pronouns have truly functioned as metaphors, opening up, rather than closing down, the imagination.

Those who in spite of linguistic and social changes continue to use generic speech are arguing a contemporary issue in archaic sentences. To chronicle the history of the language and the happenstance of grammar is one thing. But to reject developing speech patterns, to perpetuate archaic androcentrisms and label as heretics those who avoid the male pronoun suggests a misogyny perhaps so deep as to be unconscious. Those who search for an inclusive liturgical language are confident that the words of the Christian faith are not irrevocably androcentric, as was the generic speech of past English usage, and that replacements with new speech, although slow, are proceeding apace.

4 Symbolic Imagery

Why so much symbolic imagery?

Liturgical language relies extensively on symbolic imagery to carry its meaning. A symbol is something concrete that represents simultaneously many interpretive layers of something abstract. A traffic signal is not a symbol, for its meaning is univocal and its method bare. By contrast, language about heaven is symbolic. Heaven is a mental image that evokes a host of meanings: the land where the deity dwells; divine peace beyond life's troubles; the conquest of death; a state of perfection enjoyed through proximity to God. The Gospel of Matthew says "heaven" when it means "God." The complex abstract idea of life with God is represented by the multivalent symbol of heaven.

The reason symbolic language is so significant in the liturgy is that religion is to a considerable degree about the great abstractions in human life. What is the evil that is devouring the land or destroying our people or ruining my life? What is the good from which we receive life, with which we oppose evil, and to which I hope to be heading? The different religions of the world offer varying answers to these questions. But even two Christians worshipping side by side, or one Christian on two different days, see different aspects of the pervasive though amorphous "evil" and "good."

One way to define religion is to say that it is a system of symbols shared by a community of faith and practice. In the Christian tradition, doctrinal discussions have set out parameters of meaning to symbolic imagery. Christians have a smaller range of interpretation open to them than for example Hindus. But the liturgy does not intend to be narrow, as is a cult, where symbols have closed up into univocal signs like traffic signals, the single meaning of which is dictated by the authorities. Christians can walk along together using the symbolic imagery in the liturgy; the curbs keep the faithful on the road, yet the width of the highway gives us all plenty of room.

The central symbolic images of Christian liturgy derive from the Bible. Many of these images were appropriated from previous religious systems or contemporaneous social patterns. With all this variety at the source of liturgical language, we ought not be surprised that it presents many quandaries to contemporary Christians. Who determines how great a range of interpretative meaning is legitimate? When is the archaism of a symbol part of its attraction and power, and when does its past disqualify it for current use? Are phrases like "the kingdom of God" or "the man born blind" brilliant metaphor, open to layers of meaning, or obsolete imagery, not inclusive enough for contemporary consciousness?

Let us warm up to our task by considering a minor symbol of good, "the portion." Found in the Hebrew Scriptures and echoing in the Psalter, the portion was that piece of property in the Holy Land which God promised to allot to the previously landless tribe of Levi. They need be homeless no longer. Not only did God promise to give a portion: in Psalms 16 and 19, God's very self becomes our portion, the security we long for, the homeland the people need. Many contemporary translations of the Psalter retain the word "portion," while others judge its meaning obscure and substitute other words. Should we say "portion"? "homeland"? "birthright"? "inheritance"? Does it matter if a symbol that is rarely used is inaccessible to most worshippers? In the Psalter, the image is inclusive: God's gift to the Levites is promised to all Jews, and when Christians pray the psalms, to all Christians. But if not comprehended, can the symbol function inclusively?

Although this essay cannot consider every single instance of symbolic imagery in the liturgy, several of the most significant symbols can be examined, and proposals for current dilemmas suggested. This chapter will consider first "the kingdom of God," the symbolic image taken from ancient Near East politics and paramount in Christian preaching, and second "the body of Christ," the image Paul derived from Hellenistic philosophy that is essential to our understanding of the eucharist. As with good, so with evil: more images of evil are found in the liturgy than can be probed here. To work through the issues, we will examine, third, the Easter Vigil's language about "Egypt," which arose from Jewish memory of its own history, and, fourth, baptismal repudiation of "blindness," an image shared with the poetry of many cultures.

Proclaiming "the kingdom of God"

According to the Synoptic Gospels, Jesus came proclaiming the kingdom of God. The New Testament letters and John's Gospel also indicate the importance, if not the centrality, of this phrase as a summary of Christ's preaching. It remains paramount in the Church's liturgical language. The Sunday readings, focusing on the gospel selection, are chosen to proclaim this kingdom. The preaching, by explicating the readings, uses the language of "the kingdom" to make Christ available. The classic hymn "Gloria in excelsis," the creedal image of the Son at the right hand of the Father, all prayer language of Christ's reign, the theme of the prayer Jesus taught, and countless of the Church's favorite hymns rely on the imagery of the kingdom of God. The Trinitarian formulation of the fourth century is rooted in the language that the king has sent a son to rule; baptismal anointing, kneeling in prayer, and elaborate processions recall royal ritual; the architectural design of many churches, in which the table has mutated into a throne on a dais, reflects the royal metaphor; the Christological festivals of Ascension and the Reign of Christ make explicit the royal symbolism evident also in Advent, Epiphany, Passion Sunday, Good Friday, and the feast of the Holy Cross.

This way of articulating God's mercy was appropriated by Christians from the Jews, who borrowed it from the political systems of their neighbors. Demonstrating a pattern that occurred in many places and times throughout human history, the urban cultures of the ancient Near East had evolved into city states ruled by powerful men whose authority was underwritten by the gods.[41] In many of these societies, legend told of the first king vanquishing an evil monster and being rewarded by the deity with a hereditary throne. Some cultures annually reenacted the primordial battle and enthronement, the communal ritual reinvigorating the power of the legend. Since the king represented the deity to the people and appealed to the deity for the people, the well-being of the city state depended on the connection between the king and the deity.

The problems arising for contemporary Christian use of this ancient political myth are evident. Although the myth does not articulate accurate theology—God is not a male deity rewarding a superhuman warrior with absolute authority over a dependent population—"the kingdom of God" is imaginally captivating enough that the Church forgets the "No" required of all metaphoric speech. The totalitarianism implied by the myth works against mature political responsibility: neither in the political sphere nor in the spiritual life are answers readily available through helpless appeal to authority. Many commentators suggest that the myth is irretrievably androcentric. Some Christians suggest further that the idea of authority is less befitting Christian life than a pattern of creative cooperation, humans with one another and together with God.

Can contemporary proclamation of "the kingdom of God" be metaphorically life-giving and richly inclusive? Some Christians say no. The tasks following from such a judgment are massive, as our partial list of liturgical uses of the kingdom symbol makes apparent. It may be that total rejection of everything implied by "the kingdom" would alter Christianity beyond recognition.

Another way exists. Religious traditions must continuously reinterpret their symbols for an ever-changing situation. If the symbol cannot expand and change, the community will have to resist change so as to maintain the power of the symbol. But through the centuries, creative preachers and teachers, aware that the community is indeed changing, have reexamined the symbols for their healthy roots, cultivating what will thrive, tearing out what is dying. The challenge is to separate what is dying from what is thriving in this ancient political image.

We are well aware of the living power of this symbol. At each election, democracies are prey to this ancient notion that with the right leader in charge, all will be well. Indeed, perhaps the archaism of this myth is part of its allure, as the daily news demonstrates the fragility of more contemporary schemes for social well-being. The infantilism that the image might foster must be countered by the Christian adaptation of image itself: if by their baptism all Christians reign, then all share in both the privileges and the responsibilities of royalty. Were each candidate baptized with as much ritual splendor as a bishop is consecrated, then the Church would be harnessing the symbol's power for its specific Christian use.

The androcentrism of "kingdom," although a serious current obstacle, is not essential to the symbol. Indeed, in some ancient cultures, the deity who adopted the conqueror as son was the king of the universe, while in others the deity was queen. It is true that some feminists suggest that no true woman would be queen, that an image of absolute authority is inherently more male than female. This argument represents a maximizing mentality, which in maximizing gender difference assigns such things as authority to males. Minimizers find these assumptions grounded in cultural stereotypes, impossible to prove and ultimately as limiting as classical androcentrism. Thus for minimizers, God can be queen or king, no more one than the other. Application of this language to our God, however, ought best to be nongender-specific. The words sovereign and monarch are possible replacements for king; reign, dominion, and commonwealth retranslate kingdom. Images of Christ will give us quite enough male imagery: we can no longer defend its use for God.

Forming ''the body of Christ''

''The body of Christ'' is the central image for the Eucharist itself and for that assembly formed by the Eucharist. This language, recalled by the Synoptics in their narration of the last supper, is the primary metaphor Paul uses to teach the faith. It is a multivalent symbol: God is incarnate in Christ's body; Christ is available to us in the bread, which is recognized to be Christ's body; by consuming the loaf, the assembly becomes the body of Christ; each member of the body is a necessary part of the whole, just as each bite of bread is of the loaf, and as Christ is of God. ''The body of Christ,'' says the minister, as the bread forms us into Christ and so into God.

Scholars conjecture that Paul derived the image of the body of Christ from current Hellenistic philosophy. An image used by many classical authors especially in describing social reality, ''the body'' suggests unity and interdependence while requiring inclusivity and diversity. ''The body'' is easily grasped by a child; open to profound Christian mystery; useful for discussions of Christology, sacramental theology, and ecclesiology; and available for wider contemplation of ecological issues.[42] ''The body of Christ'' is as contemporary as it is ancient, much more inclusive than the image of ''the family of God,'' and not androcentric: indeed, much of the Church's iconographic tradition depicted the body of Christ as a majestic female. ''The body of Christ'' appears to be a model of liturgical language, metaphoric and inclusive.

Conquering "Egypt"

Symbolic imagery for evil raises more controversial issues than does symbolic imagery for good. All Christians would agree that insufficiency, evil, sorrow, and death exist in the natural order and in human life. But in order to symbolize evil, one selects a particular entity or experience or condition and exaggerates and intensifies the evil therein. The complex truth within the image is ignored so that the evil side can project itself. A snake is, after all, an interesting creation of God's design, neither more nor less good or evil than countless other creatures. Whether a religious system glorifies the snake as the symbol of renewal and eternal life or demonizes it as the symbol of temptation and death, descriptive accuracy about the snake has been sacrificed for a role the snake can play in human imagination. This belongs to the nature of metaphor, which will inevitably focus on only one side of any entity invoked.

In a time extremely sensitive to any negative stereotyping, appropriating anything as a symbol of evil raises criticism. "Leper" is no longer an acceptable derogatory term. People who live in cold climates may not appreciate "winter" functioning as a symbol of death. Historians may nuance popular use of "Hitler" as a name for ultimate evil. Our justifiable concern not to belittle others is further complicated by a contemporary optimism which minimizes the power and pervasiveness of evil in the world. If we are careful not to call anything evil, either because we wish not to offend or because we do not find evil in many places, Christian liturgical language will be tongue-tied. For Christian liturgy does see evil and points it out, and it has traditionally used metaphoric images to propel its speech.

The word "Egypt" provides an example of this problem. Jewish memory, recalling that its past contained a period of oppression and terror, uses the word Egypt to signify not only historic political injustice but the perennial powers of evil and death. In the Hebrew Scriptures, narratives tell of the escape from Egypt, and prophets and psalms use "Egypt" as shorthand to denote the reality of evil. However, scholars contend that Egyptian records contain no indication that Hebrew memories are historically accurate. Extensive ancient court documents make no mention of any Pharaoh enslaving peoples for forced labor. Also, those Christians and non-Christians who are contemporary residents of Egypt may find the negative symbolism irritating, if not offensive.

In the Jewish tradition, the image of "Egypt" is somewhat ambivalent. At the Passover seder, drops of wine are removed from everyone's cup in sorrow over the sufferings of the Egyptians, and the Talmud says that God stopped the joyous angelic song at the Red Sea in divine sorrow and regret at the effect of the punishment meted out.[43] But Christian liturgy is not concerned with the ambivalence possible within the image, since ultimate death, for which Egypt stands, is not ambivalent. Christians incorporate this negative imagery into their liturgy and, especially at the Easter Vigil, celebrate the destruction of Egypt's forces as a way of honoring the resurrection of Christ. According to Christian liturgical speech, God slaughtered Egypt's army to free the slaves just as God conquered the death that had bound Jesus in the grave. Use of phrases like "Pharaoh's army" or "Pharaoh's might" lessen the crisis, since "Pharaoh" does not name a contemporary reality.

The word "Babylon" functions in a similar way in Christian speech, but it occurs rarely, and since there is no contemporary political entity called Babylon, the use of the term to designate evil raises no contemporary political issues. More like "Egypt" are those passages in the Hebrew Scriptures that define the borders of the Promised Land in explicit geophysical terms, since current international politics renders these passages at least problematic, if not volatile. Other such terms are "Israel," "Judah," "Jacob," and "Ephraim." There are also the Philistines, who archeology suggests were in fact a technologically and artistically advanced people, rather than the barbarous oafs of popular imagery.

This dilemma pushes our face into the stark truth. Christian liturgical language is its own system of discourse. Paul Ricoeur teaches that no word, not even "Egypt," has meaning outside of context. In some contexts, "Egypt" denotes the ancient evil destroyed by religious faith; in other contexts, it denotes a contemporary country in Africa. Christian liturgy utilizes a sophisticated vocabulary, some terms readily accessible to the newcomer but many others, for example "the Trinity," requiring careful catechesis. The possibility, even probability, of misunderstanding must be taken seriously, and catechesis increased; but fear of an elitist tone ought not suggest that a primer vocabulary replace complex religious language. Synonyms, for example "Pharaoh's horses and riders," must be used to clarify meaning. But just as the liturgy cannot run naively away from the power of evil, so the liturgy ought not hesitate to claim its own vocabulary.

Curing "blindness"

Blindness has been used as a metaphor since the earliest literary masterpieces and mythic tales throughout the world.[44] One can cite examples from antiquity in Europe, the Near East, India, Africa, and the Orient. From Homer through the Greek tragedies, blindness functioned repeatedly not only as an example of physical disability, but also as a symbol of either one's own folly or one's fated calamity, thus either error or loss.[45] Blindness was described as an ultimate disaster: when Oedipus appears on stage blinded, the chorus says, "It would have been better to die than to live in blindness."[46] Indeed, in ancient Greece and Rome, infants born blind were usually exposed.[47] The literary tradition perpetuated the symbol of sightlessness to the present day. The concluding cantos of Dante's *Divine Comedy* rely on the images of blindness and sight to convey the Beatific Vision; [48] in T. S. Eliot's "The Waste Land," the poet's eyes fail and blind Tiresias typifies doom.[49]

The Bible shares this tradition. In some of the psalms, illness and physical debility are construed as punishment for sin. In the prophets, such images convey the reduced state of those distant from God. Blindedness is one of the physical conditions that prohibit a man from serving as priest (Lev 21:16-24), and the oracles promise that the Messiah's reign will bring sight to the blind (Isa 35:5). When John the Baptist's disciples ask whether Jesus is the Messiah, the sign that "those who are blind receive their sight" is offered as proof. In the New Testament blindness is not so much a sign of sin—recall Jesus' statement in John 9 that the man's sightlessness is not punishment—but the more essential condition of human need for the divine.

This use of blindness as a symbolic image enters liturgical language as well. The story from John 9 of the man born blind determines some of the language of the Church's annual catechesis. Other narratives of the healing of blindness occur as gospel readings. Hymns repeat the image: "I once was blind, but now I see," sings out the much-loved "Amazing Grace." By extension, all imagery of night, the condition within which no one can see, suggests blindness. The Easter Vigil ritualizes this image, and the candle at the font and at the casket recalls it.

However, several contemporary tendencies have called use of this age-old image into question. Increasingly, language is taken as functioning literally, as having in the first place factual rather than

metaphoric referents. A fairy tale about a wicked stepmother is analyzed as referring explicitly to real stepmothers, perhaps even per-
sonally to specific women who are stepmothers. To the extent that
literalness crowds out metaphor, that blindness means solely reti-
nal dysfunction, the image does not effectively convey human need.

But a second serious issue enters our conversation. Increasingly,
groups of American marked by what was traditionally described as
a disability are rejecting the implied stereotype of weakness and are
claiming their condition as a positive characteristic. According to this
mentality, blindness ought not to function as an image, surely never
as a preeminent example, of human loss and need. This mentality
is so strong that sometimes a deaf couple will seek abortion for a
fetus that is not hearing-impaired; they judge deafness to be a preferable life option. Thus not only is there no consensus on acceptable
terminology for such human conditions: there is not even consensus
that these conditions constitute disability.

Seeking advice from people with these conditions does not clarify the discussion. Some Christians who are blind, deaf, or lame
readily describe their condition as loss and are glad for the larger
community to present the condition symbolically. Other Christians
are irate at the links between their condition and human need and
judge any symbolic use as the worst stereotyping, unhelpful in society and inappropriate in liturgical speech. They argue that the image of blindness as a sign of human need excludes them, since they
reject the implied equation, and they find the opposing opinions of
sighted persons patronizing.

In thinking through a decision about use of language like ''blindness,'' the first step is to acknowledge the difficulties therein. We
must be aware that this imagery, no different from any other imagery, will not automatically serve any symbolic purpose for some
people. Since no symbolic imagery works perfectly for all, it is good
that a great variety of images is available. Since sensibilities vary,
one's own worshipping assembly must be heard concerning its
preferences and leanings.

Obviously offensive renderings must be discarded. For example,
lectionary use must replace the old word ''dumb'' with ''mute'' or
''without speech.'' The condition must never become the entire person. Thus ''the blind'' should be replaced with ''those who are
blind,'' or some such expression which does not limit the person
by the condition. Homilies and catechesis must never use the image to suggest stupidity. Most important, inspired by the dialogue

in John 9, Christians ought never construe disabilities as examples of punishment. Selections from the Psalter appointed in the lectionary must be scrutinized for that ancient notion, rejected by Christian theology, that specific cases of human need are direct punishment meted out by God.

One hopes that care in the use of such imagery will guarantee its continued use, for the liturgy needs language to speak the Christian belief that human life is not the embodied image of God that Genesis 1 describes and the eschaton promises. Christian gratitude for creation and acknowledgment of death suggest that loss can indeed be named as loss, that our universal condition is less than God intended or desires. A range of such imagery is available: illness, such as leprosy; disability, such as blindness; infirmity, such as old age; deprivation, such as poverty; helplessness, such as childhood. All that renders human life painful, all that isolates persons from the wider community, all that inhibits individuals from productive lives, all that augurs inevitable death: we need these images as inclusive metaphors to function as the foil for the promises of God.

5 Theological Language

Theology in and out of the liturgy

Theology is reasoned speech about the divine. In the Christian tradition, not all theological speech enters the liturgy. Some remains in philosophically-oriented books or scholarly investigations, not to influence, surely never to be incorporated into, the vocabulary of the assembly's praise and petition. Other theology has greatly influenced at least some Christian speech. The phrase "true God from true God, begotten, not made" in the Nicene creed represents the theological formulation of particularly Greek minds in the fourth century. Another example is the reliance of the intercessory prayer in the 1559 Book of Common Prayer on the royal metaphor for God.

Liturgy is slow to incorporate theology, for good reason. Theology expresses one way to reason out the connections between biblical words, apostolic affirmations, and human thought. Any particular theology will be unique to the culture, the time period, the education level, the worldview, the language of the Christian thinker, and will be more or less accessible to others. Since liturgy hopes to be more inclusive than any specific theological formulation, its speech about God tends to be biblical, that is, rooted in the origins of the faith. Even denominational idiosyncracies in liturgy are similarly rooted in the community's origins or self-identity. As liturgical historians remind us, the creed, an exercise in theology, is a late and optional addition to the Sunday liturgy.

Yet the liturgy cannot rest contentedly in what some think of as an immutable vocabulary. The theology of the Church is dynamic, as is each language in which Christians pray. Which language about God is in the liturgy, which not, and why; whether current decisions have been wisely made; whether change is desirable or necessary: these remain continual questions for the faithful.

Circumlocution

Scholars of language call circumlocution a figure of speech that, rather than locating exactly, talks around. As if precision is impossible, circumlocution requires extra words to circle around, demarcating a perimeter rather than defining the center. The tendency in Christian speech toward circumlocution for God illustrates the wisdom of mystics, whose speech about God stresses divine unknowability. God does not fit into human words or categories. Although both Judaism and Christianity have faith in the mercy of an accessible deity, both acknowledge that finally God's essence cannot be spoken. Contemporary Jewish liturgy exemplifies this belief when calling God "the Eternal One" or "the Name." The Gospel of Matthew demonstrates this tendency in Christianity when, to circumvent the word "God," the phrase "the kingdom of heaven" is introduced.

It is not an exaggeration to say that the most significant theological term in Christian liturgy is the word Lord. A quick review of the linguistic history of the term is useful. Originally the name of a deity in the eastern Sinai, YHWH came into the Hebrew tradition connected with the story of the burning bush as the personal name of Israel's God. Scholarly consensus suggests the word means something like "I am who I will be." Increasingly this name came to be revered as denoting a mystery beyond human speech, and faithful Jews substitute for it the circumlocution Adonai, which is the metaphor "master." By the first century, the Greek translation of Adonai, Kyrios, was used to denote either God or any male authority. Early Christian writings came to articulate the faith by means of this circumlocution. Because God is Kyrios and Jesus is Kyrios, increasingly Christians said that Jesus is God. Henceforth prayers to God as "Lord" were offered through Christ "our Lord," and in the greeting of "the peace of the Lord" the Trinitarian liturgy did not need clearly to distinguish between the creator of the universe and the Sunday appearance of the risen Christ. This Adonai/Kyrios became Dominus in Latin, Hlāf-weard in Anglo-Saxon, and Lord in modern English.

There is history not only to the name YHWH, but also to the word *lord.* In the socio-economic categories of Middle English, a lord was a wealthy landowner who to some degree dictated the lives of the poor who worked the land. In Britain today, the House of Lords retains power to delay the dictates of the House of Commons. In the United States, the status of lords was rejected and in secular use the word became either an archaic category or a pejorative term. The question Christians debate in the present is whether *Lord* can continue to convey any sacred resonance in spite of its loss of social significance and its androcentric connotation. Some say that its abandonment in secular vocabulary enhances its ability to function theologically. The first volume of *An Inclusive-Language Lectionary* of the 1980s attempted to replace the circumlocution "LORD/Lord" with another—"SOVEREIGN ONE/the Sovereign"—but vociferous objection especially by African American Christians meant the reintroduction of "LORD/Lord" in subsequent volumes.[51] While some Christians remain unaware of this controversy, and others deem it radical foolishness, continued use of "LORD/Lord" has driven some people away from regular participation at the liturgy.

As always, one can begin by detecting problems with the extreme positions in the argument. To claim that the English word *lord* is a God-given term uniquely expressing the God of faith is to ignore the fact that the word stands in a long history of linguistic decisions, each influenced by the culture of the Christians effecting the translation. To take refuge in the opposite extreme, that a term appropriate for the man Jesus is inappropriate for the non-gendered God, is to rob Trinitarian theology of its Christological keystone: that the Church in reflecting on the resurrection saw the necessity to speak of Christ as God.

Since liturgical language intends to be the middle path on which the majority can walk together, a compromise position is recommended. Some use of "LORD/Lord" will be retained, but with hopes that catechesis will educate the faithful as to its meanings. For example, Bible study should make clear the significance of the two different uses of capital letters. Overuse is to be avoided. Substitutions can be made: "The peace of Christ be with you" is the intended greeting on the day of the resurrection. Intercessory prayers can find alternate responses, such as "O gracious God, hear us." Merely replacing "Lord" with "God" constricts the text: it is better to use scriptural adjectives to elaborate the phrase than merely to eliminate offending terms. Yet another option is to translate YHWH as "The Living One," so as to stress its I AM meaning, and to render "the risen Christ" as "the Living One."[52] In this translation, life, rather than male authority, is the divinity shared and the power proclaimed.

The hope is that metaphoric circumlocutions will help immensely to counterbalance the Church's androcentric divine vocabulary. God is our Portion. God is our Cup. We are leaning on the Everlasting Arms. God's face will shine upon us. The circumlocutions, in their inclusivity, are appropriate in honoring God.

Catachresis

Catachresis is a term rhetoricians use to denote an admittedly inappropriate word forced into new usage because an appropriate word is unavailable. Theology must admit that it often relies on catachresis. Indeed, to speak of divinity with human speech, words will of necessity be misused or reused for specific religious meaning. Thus just as the Christian mystics free liturgy for circumlocution, systematicians offer liturgy catachresis, words not quite right, some actually quite wrong, but baptized to fill the semantic lacunae in human speech.

The fundamental catachresis in liturgical speech is Trinitarian language. There is a customary way for human speech to talk about a transcendent deity. But a transcendent deity who became incarnate in a specific man and who now lives manifest in human community, a unity in which three expressions are eternally active and without hierarchy: this is extremely difficult to say. Into our semantic lacuna comes help from several sources: the ancient Near Eastern myth of the victorious son of the gods; an erroneous biology which postulated that the father was the sole source of life; the Hellenistic idea of an emanating Logos; an assortment of biblical passages of varying origins, intent, and vocabulary; and the Church's lived experience as itself a vehicle for and container of God. Current discussion must consider these various contexts and the ''wrong'' words the Church borrowed from them. Not only are these words inadequate to articulate multiformed mercy, but they are prone to misunderstanding, since their current secular connotations or their original usage are in all likelihood more accessible than their technical theological meaning.

Current examination of the androcentric language in liturgy has demonstrated that ''Father'' and ''Son'' terminology has been both misunderstood by the faithful and mistaught by the Church's teachers. It cannot be denied that this language has often sanctified patriarchy, the amorphous nature of "Spirit" unable to overpower the male connotations of "Father and Son." The argument has raged in the United States at least since the mid-nineteenth century, when Elizabeth Cady Stanton, judging Trinitarian language too androcentric to be helpful to women, became a Deist,[53] while Sarah Grimke, in defending the Bible as essentially liberating for women, assumed its androcentric extremes to be mistranslations and human misstatements of the gospel.[54]

Although some in the Church have donned blinders or protest that even the questions are evidence of heresy, many theologians from around the world are probing ways to reform the Church's use of Trinitarian speech. It is true that many naive proposals follow Stanton and replace Trinitarianism with Deism. But others assume that the truth of God is deeper than our words, and are engaged in a sympathetic study of the origins of divine metaphors, of their negative as well as positive connotations throughout the Church's history, and of the sense the language currently conveys of either grace or silliness.[55] In what contexts can the speech "Father, Son, Spirit" be the road of the wideness of God's mercy? While "Father, Son, Spirit" remains the narrow center of the path, the Church needs to find other metaphors helpful in broadening the path, in giving us all some shoulder room. These metaphors are being found in the Bible and in the Church's fathers and mothers, as well as being written newly by living theologians.

One example of the attempts to add other metaphors to our descriptions of God and so increase the inclusivity of our speech is seen in the current interest in Sophia. A growing list of Christian writers, in presenting the pre-biblical and biblical history of this term and its occasional use in Christian history, argue its attractiveness for our time.[56] The image offers our sexually laden speech a refreshing androgyny, for while Sophia is herself the great wise woman, the quality wisdom is not stereotypically the province of females and their anatomy. Wisdom rules heaven and earth, and so, like optimal language for Christ, reaches beyond gender designation to point to humanity renewed in God. Yet "Wisdom" is another example of catachresis: Jesus is not that goddess of wisdom in whom we in fact no longer believe.

Circumlocution and catachresis come together in the Aaronic blessing from Numbers 6. Here the Living One blesses and keeps us; the face of God shines graciously on us; and we receive from the Living God grace and peace. This biblical petition expresses the Trinity no less than classic Trinitarian language, albeit in alternate words. In the Hebrew text of this blessing, God is named YHWH: how we come to translate this into American English will require catachresis. Also, the benediction relies on circumlocution, for it evokes God's face and cites the mercy that flows from God, rather than attempting to name God's very essence. Deciding on a translation of this ancient benediction exemplifies the Church's continuing tasks in talking about God in the liturgy.

6 The Householder's Treasure

In Matthew 13, after telling the people seven parables, Jesus likens the teacher to a householder whose storeroom contains treasure that is both new and old. This is a typically Matthean comment for Jesus to make, for the Gospel of Matthew itself regularly mixes language and imagery from the old Jewish tradition with the new revelation of God in Jesus, using the old to say the new, altering the old by the new, contrasting the old with the new. In this same way liturgical language must always honor the old and be open to the new, judging both alike for their metaphoric nature and their inclusive character.

What is old

One final example of an old treasure in the liturgical storeroom that is worth keeping is the image of the devil. Some liturgical revisors have viewed this imagery as hopelessly archaic, crushed by centuries of art and layers of nonsense so as to be no longer useful for the contemporary mind. The primitive nature of a personification of evil has suggested to some that the metaphor be demythologized. Yet the immense popularity of monster movies demonstrates that vast numbers of people respond to such a metaphor of evil. Our terror before the inexplicable power of evil deserves liturgical expression, and the old imagery of the devil can assist in this task.

Many mythologies give divine or semi-divine status to troublemakers, but it was most likely ancient Persian dualism that bequeathed to Judaism and then Christianity a single evil being. Christianity tempered the dualism with its theological assertion that God's power is always greater than Satan's, and the Church's emphasis on personal culpability meant that the devil is never to be blamed for our sin. But Satan has proven a useful metaphor, a way to put evil into our minds, to introduce it to children, to give shape to its monstrous unbelievability, to confront its destructive might. Of course, as with any religious metaphor, its presentation can degenerate into superficiality; a puny image of evil can imply that sin and death are merely minor annoyances, not to be taken seriously. But that a metaphor has been marred in the past does not demand that it be discarded. The householder can refurbish it anytime.

Care must be taken, however, to avoid the stereotypes of evil that determined the depictions of the devil in previous centuries. The devil cannot be black, as Europeans often imagined; or female, as many depictions of the serpent in Eden's tree suggested; or male, as historic patriarchy assumes of all powerful figures. Perhaps the devil is best "it," although eager to be incarnated into any "he" or "she" around.

On the other hand, an example of an old treasure which must be discarded is the identification of black with evil. Dirty versus clean, night versus day, dark versus light: these remain metaphoric options for liturgical language. Perhaps there are cultures where skin color is not coded to social status; perhaps American speech will wholly replace designation of skin tone with labels of ethnic origin. But while "white" and "black" still denote human beings whose skin color determines their social approval, the Church cannot use "black" as an adjective suggesting human evil or divine displeasure and "white" for the opposite.[57]

What is new

Not all problematic imagery comes down from the past. Current freedom to incorporate contemporary imagery into the liturgy, into its homilies, hymns, and intercessions, if not yet into the ordinary of the Eucharist, requires perpetual vigilance. An example of a new image which is liturgically precarious is the extremely popular language of the personal journey.

The personal journey is newly a reality for many contemporary people, as more people live alone than ever before in history. The United States gives considerable focus to the individual: the backpacker can afford to walk across Alaska, the seeker can wander through world religions, and weekly therapy can assist persons in a psychological journey within the mind. One thinks, for example, of Joseph Campbell's myth series, in which the personal journey is the primary metaphor for a respectable human life.[58]

The image has not been a traditional Christian symbol. In the Scriptures, people journeyed together. The entire clan migrated. The evangelists traveled two by two. Although Elijah walked alone for forty days, the lonely prophet is a poor image of the Christian, for whom the journey is meant to be communal. Even Camaldolese monks assemble for prayer: the mountain of God is here in our midst. The great dangers of the image of the personal journey are its denial of the community, its glorification of private perceptions over the assembly's shared life, and its assumption of an affluent lifestyle filled with individual options. The liturgy cannot mindlessly incorporate contemporary images as though their very inclusion renders Sunday liturgy relevant. The question must always be whether the new image brilliantly incarnates the Christian gospel or whether it distorts the faith beyond recognition.

However, one image we can gladly welcome into Christian liturgy is the tree of life. Found in ancient cultures, alive through centuries of art, important in the iconography of many religions, and newly popular as a symbol of wholeness, the tree of life has only a meager history in Western liturgical texts. Although the Bible begins and concludes with the tree of life image, most biblical references to a sacred tree are pejorative, for the Israelites were enjoined to reject worship in groves of trees and the Asherah tree of the Canaanite goddess. Added to the biblical bias was European Christianity's inheritance from Greek thought: a disdain for nature and a preference for the disembodied. Beyond Fortunatus's hymns which honor the cross, *Vexilla regis* and *Pange, lingua*, liturgical language contains few references to this mythic metaphor of divine life. However, an increasing number of new hymns are based on the tree of life image, and since hymnody is an important first step toward incorporation of imagery in the liturgy,[59] one can assume that the tree of life will enjoy renewed life in the Church.

At least some gems

An issue concerning liturgical language that is often the focus of controversy is the matter of stylistic excellence. Some discarded classic liturgical texts were gems of prose or poetry, multifaceted pieces of brilliance. However, not all older texts were literary masterpieces. Indeed, our judging the superiority of older versus newer texts is made difficult because of another characteristic of superior liturgy: that it be known by heart, its edges rubbed off by decades or centuries of editing, its center reflecting the community's own history of sorrow and joy. As symphony orchestras know all too well, audiences clap louder for pieces they know, perhaps applauding their own knowledge as much as the musicians' performance. Separating out the well-beloved from the stylistically excellent is not an easy task.

We cannot forget, either, that traditional language can be cherished for the wrong reasons. Like many modern European languages, Middle English had two words for "you," the informal, intimate "thou," and the formal, distant "you," and social stability required that people use these terms correctly. Indeed, early Quakers were jailed for practicing their ideals of equality by boldly addressing magistrates as "thou." Christian prayer chose to address God as "Thou," since God, like one's spouse, was intimate, close, dear. Some twentieth-century conservatives, ignorant of this history, vociferously defended "Thou" as more clearly demonstrating the magisterial distance of the divine from the human suppliant. We have perhaps no better example of how each word in our liturgical vocabulary has its own history of appropriate and inappropriate connotations.

The goal of liturgical language is to use the finest vernacular, to find the most intellectually and emotionally captivating words and phrases to speak of God and to articulate the human condition. Lesser language will finally fail. We cannot fool ourselves: perfecting the liturgy in a certain linguistic style, contemporary U.S. English for example, is a daunting task, requiring great writers and wise editors, individual efforts and the communities' corrections. Christians will not agree about what constitutes appropriate liturgical prose, about whether the syntax is too rudimentary or too elaborate, the vocabulary too simplistic or too esoteric. The process since midcentury of finding a U.S. English style for Christian liturgy has been heartening, however, for there is considerable evidence that liturgical language is decade by decade gaining stylistic excellence. There are indeed some jewels in the treasure chest.

At the conclusion of Matthew 13, Jesus asks the disciples if they have comprehended the metaphors in his parables. They blithely answer yes: the reader recognizes this as typically Matthean, complimenting the disciples with total understanding. However, Matthew's confident narrative is flanked historically by the first Gospel, Mark, in which the disciples understand practically nothing, and the fourth Gospel, John, in which the mystery of the incarnation shines as an incomprehensible light.

Liturgical language attempts to put into words the mystery of the Trinity, the surprise of grace, and the reality of the inspired community. To achieve this task, the Church needs metaphors accurate enough to convey the historic faith, deep enough to contain human experience, inclusive enough to speak to many different peoples. To some of the images we are given, we respond readily; other images chafe; to these we add some images newly polished up, some newly acquired. A metaphor's age does not determine its appropriateness. Our continuous task of judging liturgical speech is more difficult than either preserving everything old or trashing the old for the new: the liturgy is neither museum nor shopping mall. Rather, the liturgy selects from the shelves of the Church's storehouses those inclusive metaphors that for this decade, perhaps for this century, best say mercy. All the wisdom—although not all the grousing—of all the faithful is welcomed to this task.

Endnotes

1. For discussions of liturgical language, see Ian T. Ramsey, *Religious Language: An Empirical Placing of Theological Phrases* (New York: Macmillan, 1957); Daniel B. Stevick, *Language in Worship: Reflections on a Crisis* (New York: Seabury, 1970); and A. C. Thiselton, *Language, Liturgy and Meaning,* Grove Liturgical Studies 2 (Bramcote, Notts.: Grove Books, 1975).

2. Wallace Stevens, *Opus Posthumous,* ed. Samuel French Morse (New York: Knopf, 1966) 221.

3. Emily Dickinson, ''640,'' in *The Complete Poems of Emily Dickinson,* ed. Thomas H. Johnson (Boston: Little, Brown and Company, 1957) 317.

4. See Frederick R. Karl, *William Faulkner: American Writer* (New York: Weidenfeld & Nicolson, 1989) 118.

5. Thomas Aquinas, *Summa Theologiae* 1.13.

6. See for example J. A. DiNoia, O.P., ''Knowing and Naming the Triune God: The Grammar of Trinitarian Confession,'' in *Speaking the Christian God: The Holy Trinity and the Challenge of Feminism,* ed. Alvin F. Kimel, Jr. (Grand Rapids: Eerdmans, 1992) 162–87.

7. See Roland M. Frye, ''Language for God and Feminist Language: Problems and Principles,'' in Kimel, *Speaking the Christian God,* 17–43.

8. See for example John L. Farthing, *Thomas Aquinas and Gabriel Biel: Interpretation of St. Thomas Aquinas in German Nominalism on the Eve of the Reformation* (Durham: Duke University Press, 1988) 19–24.

9. See for example George M. Marsden, *Understanding Fundamentalism and Evangelicalism* (Grand Rapids: Eerdmans, 1991) 130–34, and Ernest R. Sanders, *The Roots of Fundamentalism: British and American Millenarianism 1800–1930* (Chicago: University of Chicago Press, 1980) 103–31.

10. Augustine, *Confessions,* tr. Henry Chadwick (Oxford: Oxford University Press, 1992) 5.14.24.

11. Paul Ricoeur, *The Rule of Metaphor: Multi-Disciplinary Studies of the Creation of Meaning in Language,* tr. Robert Czerny (Toronto: University of Toronto

Press, 1977). See also Sallie McFague, *Models of God: Theology for an Ecological, Nuclear Age* (Philadelphia: Fortress, 1987).

12. Paul Ricoeur, "The Image of God and the Epic of Man," in *History and Truth,* ed. Charles A. Kelbley (Evanston: Northwestern University Press, 1965) 127.

13. Ricoeur, *The Rule of Metaphor,* 77.

14. Wallace Stevens, "Thirteen Ways of Looking at a Blackbird," in *Collected Poems of Wallace Stevens* (New York: Knopf, 1955) 92–95.

15. Tryggve N. D. Mettinger, *In Search of God: The Meaning and Message of the Everlasting Names,* trans. Frederick H. Cryer (Philadelphia: Fortress, 1987) 24–29, 69–72.

16. Frank Moore Cross, *Canaanite Myth and Hebrew Epic* (Cambridge, Mass.: Harvard University Press, 1973) 54–55.

17. See Roland E. Murphy, O.Carm., *The Tree of Life: An Exploration of Biblical Wisdom Literature* (New York: Doubleday, 1990); and Pheme Perkins, "Sophia and the Mother-Father: The Gnostic Goddess," in *The Book of the Goddess Past and Present: An Introduction to Her Religion,* ed. Carl Olson (New York: Crossroad, 1983) 97–109.

18. Thomas E. Toon, "Old English Dialects," in *The Cambridge History of the English Language,* ed. Richard M. Hogg (New York: Cambridge University Press, 1992) 1:432–33.

19. For an original text of Julian of Norwich, see *A Revelation of Love,* ed. Marion Glasscoe (Exeter: University of Exeter Press, 1993).

20. Bill Bryson, *The Mother Tongue: English and How It Got That Way* (New York: William Morrow, 1990) 56.

21. Sarah Grimke, *Letters on the Equality of the Sexes and Other Essays,* ed. Elizabeth Ann Bartlett (New Haven: Yale University Press, 1988) 32.

22. Many such proposals are available. See for example Rosemary Radford Ruether, *Sexism and God-Talk: Toward a Feminist Theology* (Boston: Beacon, 1983); Nancy Hardesty, *Inclusive Language in the Church* (Atlanta: John Knox Press, 1987); Marjorie Proctor-Smith, *In Her Own Rite: Constructing Feminist Liturgical Tradition* (Nashville: Abington, 1990); Gail Ramshaw, *God beyond Gender: Feminist Christian God-Talk* (Minneapolis: Fortress, 1995).

23. See *The Women's Bible Commentary,* ed. Carol A. Newsom and Sharon H. Ringe (Louisville: Westminster/John Knox Press, 1992) for a book-by-book discussion of androcentrism in the Bible.

24. Elisabeth Schüssler Fiorenza, *In Memory of Her: A Feminist Theological Reconstruction of Christian Origins* (New York: Crossroad, 1988) 43–48.

25. See Casey Miller and Kate Swift, *Words and Women: New Language in New Times,* rev. ed. (San Francisco: HarperCollins, 1991) 59–75, for a discussion of such semantic polarization.

26. See for example "Guidelines for Equal Treatment of the Sexes in the McGraw-hill Book Company Publications" (McGraw-Hill, 1974); "Guidelines for Creating Positive Sexual and Racial Images in Educational Materials" (Mac-

millan, 1975); "Eliminating Stereotypes" (Houghton Mifflin, 1982); "Guidelines for Improving the Images of Women in Textbooks" (Scott, Foresman and Company, 1974).

27. A. Pace Nilsen, et al., *Sexism and Language* (Urbana, Ill.: National Council of Teachers of English, 1977) 182–91.

28. Casey Miller and Kate Swift, *The Handbook of Nonsexist Writing*, 2d ed. (New York: Harper & Row, 1980). Also *The Chicago Manual of Style*, 13th ed. (Chicago: University of Chicago Press, 1982) 61.

29. For examples see the most recently published worshipbooks of American Christians: *The United Methodist Hymnal* (Nashville: The United Methodist Publishing House, 1989); *The United Methodist Book of Worship* (Nashville: The United Methodist Publishing House, 1992); the Presbyterian *Book of Common Worship* (Louisville: Westminster/John Knox Press, 1993); and the proposed texts of the International Commission on English in the Liturgy.

30. Gregory of Nazianzus, "The Fifth Theological Oration: On the Spirit," in *A Select Library of Nicene and Post-Nicene Fathers*, ed. Philip Schaff and Henry Wace, 2d series (New York: Christian Literature Company, 1894) 5:520.

31. See for example Kari Elisabeth Børresen, "God's Image, Man's Image: Patristic Interpretation of Gen. 1:27 & 1 Cor. 11:7," in *Image of God and Gender Models in Judeo-Christian Tradition*, ed. K. A. Børresen (Oslo: Solum, 1991) 201–3.

32. Elizabeth A. Johnson, *She Who Is: The Mystery of God in Feminist Theological Discourse* (New York: Crossroad, 1992) 241–43.

33. See for example Cynthia Fuchs Epstein, *Deceptive Distinctions: Sex, Gender, and the Social Order* (New Haven: Yale University Press, 1988) 232–40.

34. See for example Robert W. Jenson, "The Father, He . . ." in Kimel, *Speaking the Christian God*, 95–109.

35. See for example Susanne Heine, *Matriarchs, Goddesses and Image of God: A Critique of a Feminist Theology*, trans. John Bowden (Minneapolis: Augsburg, 1989). For historical data, see Tikva Frymer-Kensky, *In the Wake of the Goddesses: Women, Culture, and the Biblical Transformation of Pagan Myth* (New York: Free Press, 1992) 187–88.

36. See for example Elizabeth Achtemeier, "Exchanging God for 'No Gods': A Discussion of Female Language for God," in Kimel, *Speaking the Christian God*, 1–16.

37. See for example Garrett Green, "The Gender of God and the Theology of Metaphor," in Kimel, *Speaking the Christian God*, 44–64.

38. An example in which "he" is pejorative and "she" the preferred deity is Nancy Mairs, *Ordinary Time: Cycles in Marriage, Faith, and Renewal* (Boston: Beacon, 1993) 162–63. However, an example of "she" as the divine object of our praise and even our anger is Janet Morley, "I Desire Her with My Whole Heart," in *Feminist Theology: A Reader*, ed. Ann Loades (Louisville: Westminster/John Knox Press, 1990) 162.

39. Heinrich Denziger, *The Sources of Catholic Dogma*, trans. Roy J. Deferrari (St. Louis: Herder, 1957) 171.

40. Samuel Rodigast, "Whatever God Ordains Is Right," *Lutheran Book of Worship* (Minneapolis: Augsburg Fortress, 1987) no. 446.

41. See Gerda Lerner, *The Creation of Patriarchy* (New York: Oxford University Press, 1986). For examples from many world cultures, see John Wier Perry, *Lord of the Four Quarters: The Mythology of Kingship* (New York: Paulist, 1966).

42. Sallie McFague, *The Body of God: An Ecological Theology* (Minneapolis: Fortress, 1993).

43. *Sanh.* 39b.

44. Michael E. Monbeck, *The Meaning of Blindness: Attitudes Toward Blindness and Blind People* (Bloomington: Indiana University Press, 1973) 119–38.

45. Richard E. Doyle, S.J., *Ate, Its Use and Meaning: A Study in the Greek Poetic Tradition from Homer to Euripides* (New York: Fordham, 1984) 2–4.

46. Sophocles, *Oedipus the King*, 1. 1368.

47. Monbeck, *The Meaning of Blindness*, 24.

48. Dante Alighieri, *Paradise*, cantos 26–33.

49. T. S. Eliot, "The Waste Land," in *The Complete Poems and Plays 1909–1950* (New York: Harcourt, Brace and World, 1958) 38, 44.

50. *The Book of Common Prayer 1559*, ed. John E. Booty (Washington, D.C.: Folger Shakespeare Library, 1982) 253–54.

51. *An Inclusive-Language Lectionary: Readings for Year A*, ed. Division of Education and Ministry, National Council of the Churches of Christ in the U.S.A. (Atlanta: John Knox Press, 1983).

52. Ramshaw, *God beyond Gender*, 54–57.

53. Elizabeth Cady Stanton, in *The Woman's Bible* (1898) (Seattle: Coalition Task Force on Women and Religion, 1974) 113.

54. Grimke, *Letters on the Equality of the Sexes and Other Essays*, 18.

55. See for example Ruth C. Duck, *Gender and the Name of God: The Trinitarian Baptismal Formula* (New York: Pilgrim, 1991); and Catherine Mowry LaCugna, *God for Us: The Trinity and Christian Life* (San Francisco: HarperCollins, 1991).

56. For example, Johnson, *She Who Is*, 124–87; Susan Cady, Marian Ronan, and Hal Tausig, *Wisdom's Feast: Sophia in Study and Celebration* (San Francisco: Harper & Row, 1989); Jann Aldredge-Clanton, *In Search of the Christ-Sophia: An Inclusive Christology for Liberating Christians* (Mystic, Conn.: Twenty-Third Publication, 1995); and Elisabeth Schüssler Fiorenza, *Jesus: Miriam's Child, Sophia's Prophet* (New York: Continuum, 1994).

57. For a full discussion see Dolores S. Williams, *Sisters in the Wilderness: The Challenge of Womanist God-Talk* (Maryknoll, N.Y.: Orbis, 1993) 84–107.

58. Joseph Campbell, *The Power of Myth*, with Bill Moyers (New York: Doubleday, 1988), and the popular video series.

59. See Brian Wren, *What Language Shall I Borrow? God-Talk in Worship: A Male Response to Feminist Theology* (New York: Crossroad, 1989) for a discussion of imagery in hymnody.